CHATHAM HOUSE ESSAYS: 1

THE CHINESE VIEW OF THEIR PLACE IN THE WORLD

CHATHAM HOUSE ESSAYS

It is proposed to publish under this general title short studies designed to illuminate and to provoke discussion of issues in the field of international affairs.

This is the first in the series.

The Chinese View of Their Place in the World

BY
C. P. FITZGERALD

Issued under the auspices of the
Royal Institute of International Affairs

OXFORD UNIVERSITY PRESS

LONDON   NEW YORK   TORONTO

1964

Oxford University Press, Amen House, London E.C.4

GLASGOW NEW YORK TORONTO MELBOURNE WELLINGTON
BOMBAY CALCUTTA MADRAS KARACHI LAHORE DACCA
CAPE TOWN SALISBURY NAIROBI IBADAN ACCRA
KUALA LUMPUR HONG KONG

*Printed in Great Britain by
The Bowering Press, Plymouth*

Contents

I

Pre-T'ang China

The origin of Chinese civilization

To Western man China has ever seemed to be at the ends of the earth. 'Remote and inaccessible', were the words Gibbon used to describe the Roman view of the Land of the Seres: 'Far East' still remains in common use; many clichés such as 'from China to Peru' reiterate the idea that China is the most distant of lands, the most unlike the home country. Yet in geographical terms China is not in reality 'farther' away from Europe than parts of America, or even Africa. Africa might have been 'dark', western America 'wild', but darkness could be lightened, wildernesses can be tamed: distance can never be narrowed. There was another factor, half acknowledged, in this Western view of China. There was the uneasy realization that the Chinese did not feel this way about themselves: they were not conscious of living at the ends of the earth, they even presumed to imagine that they lived at the centre. The inhabitants of Africa, America or Australia, equally distant, made no such claim, could not make it, for they were still primitive when their countries were taken over and colonized by the Europeans. The Chinese resisted such contacts, and were too numerous to be overcome; so they remained outside the Europe-centred universe, undigested, 'remote and inaccessible'. China is the only large area which has never, at any period, been brought under the rule of Western men, the only region where an alternative tradition, equally ancient, has flourished and persisted down to modern times.

That tradition, which makes China the centre of the world, is, of course, equally false in geographical terms, but for a very long period it had a practical reality for the Chinese people. They did indeed live in a closed world, of which fertile China was the centre; to the north the barren steppe, to the east the endless sea, to the west the highest mountain system in the world, southward tropical jungles. In their favoured environment they developed a civilization which owed very little to contacts with any foreign people, and had no links with any people of a similar level of development.

This view of the origin of Chinese civilization and of the Chinese people was contested by Western scholars in the nineteenth century. Diffusionism was the accepted theory of all development. The Chinese must have 'come from' somewhere, their culture must have been borrowed from some other region, their ruling class must have derived from one of those acceptable foci of early civilization, Egypt or Mesopotamia. Terrien de Lacouperie found linguistic parallels with the languages of Sumer and Akkad: the ideographic script could only have a cuneiform origin, bronze must have come from the west of Asia. Unfortunately the linguistic parallels are false, the ideographic script has no relation to hieroglyphics, and the evidence of archaeology increasingly supports the contrary view, that since early neolithic times the ancient material culture of China shows only indigenous influences. The former belief that the Chou people, who founded the kingdom of that name, had come from Central Asia, displacing the Shang, and bringing with them the higher culture of the west of Asia, has been shown to be without foundation.

Disturbingly, the Chinese, it would now appear, have always been in China; it is at least very probable that they developed the art of smelting metal themselves, as a consequence of advanced pottery techniques, and it is virtually certain that they devised the ideographic script from the practice of reading oracles from the shape of the cracks made by applying heat to bones and tortoise shell. The Chinese view of their own origins, however unscientific in its traditional expression, seems to be more consonant with the evidence of archaeology than the theories of diffusion.

The Chinese tradition is naturally strongly coloured by the ideas of later ages, when a great political and cultural union had come into existence. Yet the reverence for an ancient text and the unchanging character of the ideographic script have preserved to some extent the earlier beliefs, however much these may be explained or rationalized by later commentaries. It is clear that in the earliest literate period, the first millennium B.C., there was not one China but many kingdoms, and also barbarous tribes, regarded as alien, living in the midst of what is now North China. The south, everything from the Yangtze valley southward, was then no part of 'China', or to use the terminology of the time, 'Chung Yüan' 'the Central Plain'. It is also clear that at this remote period the process of absorbing such foreign peoples, of amalgamating small kingdoms, and expanding into sparsely inhabited areas, the process by which in historical times the Chinese empire grew, had already begun. As old as the concept of the Central Kingdom, the civilized world, is the tradition that any people who adopted the ways of that kingdom, learnt its language and submitted to its rule, were henceforward an integral part of it, members of the civilized race of men.

The circumstances of the ancient Chinese prevented the rise of the concept of nationality in the sense in which it appears at a very early period in the Western world. The Chinese distinguished between civilized and barbarous peoples, but they did not put all the latter into one category, nor did the names they gave them have the same semantic force as the term 'barbarian' had to Greeks and Latins. Northern nomadic peoples in the steppes beyond China were Jung, Ti, and later Hu. Southern forest dwellers, who were also, like the Chinese, rice cultivators, but backward, were Man: western mountain peoples from the fringes of Tibet were Chiang. At a very early period the Chinese of the Central Kingdom knew themselves as Hsia, the term 'All the Hsia' standing for the loose group of separate states, which although politically independent, were linked by culture and by language.

Behind this terminology was an economic reality. The nomadic peoples were not cultivators, the Chinese and the southern Man were not pastoralists. Therefore the southern peoples could be absorbed, civilized, made into 'Chinese', gradually admitted into the circle of the civilized states. But the northern nomads remained beyond this pale. Their steppes yielded no crops, it was profitless to conquer such a country, all that could be done was to keep its dangerous inhabitants from raiding into China. At a later period the Chinese rulers began to construct long walls along the ridges of the mountain chain which separates North China from the Mongolian steppe. Still later these earlier walls were linked together to form the Great Wall, running from the sea coast for fourteen hundred miles to the borders of the Central Asian desert. Thus a physical limit was set to the bounds of civilization, beyond which the northern nomads might live, or die, as they would; their realm was no part of China.

No such limit was imposed on southern expansion. The peoples of South China emerged at the end of the first millennium B.C. grouped, like the older North, into states, to whose rulers Chinese pedigrees were attributed, legitimizing them as now among the civilized. It was accepted, and recorded, that these southern peoples did not speak the same language as the northern peoples. Whether in truth it was a different language, or different dialects, cannot now be determined. But this fact did not make them foreign in the sense that the Chinese recognized the northern nomads as for ever alien. The contests of the warring kingdoms, north and south alike, were seen as the struggles of princely houses for supremacy, not as the conquest of one people by a foreign race. Statesmen, nobles and warriors could change their allegiance, travel the land in search of a just prince or a worthy master. This was not treachery, no sense of betraying the home country deterred men from taking service under a prince who might become the enemy of the ruler of the wanderer's native land. But few fled to the barbarians of the north, no sage expected to find just rule or moral enlightenment among the nomads. A clear distinction between the desert and the sown, between farmer and herdsman, cultivator and nomad grew among the Chinese, identified as a distinction between civilized and savage, but inapplicable to peoples of the same way of life. Nationality remained an unknown concept, patriotism, lacking the incentive of rival civilized peoples, formidable, but alien, never appeared. The noble owed loyalty to his prince, but he could change his prince. The prince strove to enlarge his dominions, but did not think of his followers as a conquering race and his enemies as aliens to be enslaved.

The unity of the Chinese world

A vague but pervasive sense of unity long preceded the first effective political unification of the Chinese world. In later times this was interpreted as a memory of the long lost union which it was believed had been established at the dawn of time by the Sage Kings of the Golden Age. Confucius and his followers firmly believed in this myth, regarding the actual political disunion of their times as a deplorable decline. The ancient historical North China kingdom of Shang, which occupied the lower Yellow River basin, was believed to have once ruled all China, and to have been itself preceded by another, even more extensive kingdom named Hsia. These names are still, in traditional history, applied to the first two 'dynasties' of China, although there is no archaeological evidence for the existence of a Hsia kingdom, and the Shang certainly did not rule beyond the present provinces of Hopei and Honan.

Early accounts, quasi-historical, claimed that the Chou, who replaced the Shang at the end of the first millennium B.C., distributed the whole of North China as fiefs to members of the royal house or to worthy followers. Many of these pedigrees are manifestly later 'legitimizations' of emergent states formerly barbarous; others may have some foundation in fact. The rulers of Chou did exercise a kind of suzerainty over the numerous princes and lesser rulers of small states. In fully historical times, from the ninth century B.C. onwards, this suzerainty was purely ceremonial and titular, but there remains uncertainty as to whether it had not been something more real in the first centuries of Chou rule, for which no detailed and wholly reliable historical record remains. It is clear that whatever the political reality may have been, there existed a general sense of cultural and racial unity between the states, expressed in the belief that all the rulers were descended from the semi-divine Sage Kings of remote antiquity.

The sense of unity, of belonging to a civilization rather than to a state or a nation, was thus very ancient. It transcended political allegiances and the strife of princes. It formed, in later times, the foundation for the acceptance by the Chinese peoples as a whole of the firm, strong and enduring centralized government which first united the country in the third century B.C. It was an ideal which could be transmitted to the southern peoples as they were absorbed by or accepted into the group of older civilized states. The southern peoples, who now form a large part of the population of South China, were not ethnically very different from the northern peoples, their way of life was similar, their customs old fashioned perhaps, but not re-pellent. In sharp contrast to the endless border warfare which raged along the line of the Great Wall throughout Chinese history, the southern peoples offered little organ-ized resistance to inclusion in the empire. This fact accen-tuated the distinction which was made between Chinese and nomads, irreconcilable foes; and Chinese and southern barbarians, who were regarded merely as backward, 'raw' country cousins. In modern times in south-west China, the expressions 'sheng' and 'shu', 'raw' and 'ripe' (or 'cooked') were still commonly used to distinguish between those non-Chinese peoples who clung to their old customs, and those who had to a great degree accepted Chinese civilization. There can be little doubt that this traditional outlook dates back 2,000 years and more, from the first expansion into the Yangtze valley.

Contacts with foreign countries

The absence of any rival centre of civilization was a factor which contributed most powerfully to the traditional Chinese view of the world. Some contact, of a very indirect kind, probably existed along the line of oases which later formed the great caravan route across Central Asia to Persia and beyond. But before the Han dynasty (206 B.C.–A.D. 221) and the foundation of the unified empire there is no Chinese record of any knowledge of the civilized peoples of western and southern Asia. The stimulus which the discovery of these countries imparted in the Han period, the importance attached to the contacts then made suggest very strongly that nothing of such countries was hitherto known, nor do the full and detailed Han records anywhere suggest that these contacts were then developed on the basis of vague or imperfect previous knowledge. It was in search of an ally, another nomadic people, who could turn the flank of his principal enemies, the Hsiung Nu nomads, that the Han Emperor Wu sent his envoy to the west, across the deserts of Sinkiang. The tribe had migrated westward, and did not wish to return, but the envoy found himself on the borders of Persia, and learned for the first time of the existence of India. Later envoys reached Persia, reported upon Rome; some may have entered the Roman Empire.

Before long Chinese armies were campaigning in what is now Russian Central Asia, and over the next two centuries the Chinese acquired a considerable knowledge of the west Asian world. The description of the Roman Empire preserved in the Han Histories, although somewhat garbled and clearly referring to events and institutions of different epochs, is yet a far fuller account than any Roman or Greek record of China that has come down to us. The Chinese recognized that they had come into contact with a people of equal civilization. They paid the Romans the compliment of calling their empire 'Ta Ts'in', which they explained as meaning 'Great Ts'in', because the people were as civilized as the Chinese themselves (Ts'in) but taller in stature, and thus 'great'. They discovered, too, that the Roman Empire was a lucrative market for Chinese silk, and promoted the trade, complaining that the Persians extorted an unfair middleman's price. They sought without success to find a route which avoided Persian control.

If the distances had been smaller, the intervening lands less hostile, and the western region more fertile, it is probable that these discoveries would have led to a continuing and closer association, both in peace and war, between

China and the Levant. Only a strong régime in China could afford to maintain armies in the deserts and rare oases of Sinkiang. The route was exposed to nomad raids from the Mongolian steppe; Persia lay across the way. It was too far: fitful contacts continued until the end of the Han Empire, revived under later strong dynasties, survived as a trade route through the centuries; but it was at best a weak, long link, liable to frequent interruption. Precious goods such as silk from China and glass from the Roman Empire were transmitted; artistic motifs and religious ideas seeped slowly into China, but the contact had no political significance, did not in any way modify the policies of statecraft, had no influence on thought or literature. The Chinese knew that the Roman world existed, they traded with it at long range, they admired what they knew, but all this had no direct bearing on their lives, made no modification in their view of the world. If today we were to receive certain proof of intelligent life in a remote planet, it is likely we could effect a closer communication with such beings than the Chinese or the Romans were able to effect with each other in the Han period.

There was also the sea route to the west. This, too, seems to have become known for the first time to the Chinese in the Han period, possibly as a direct consequence of their conquest and occupation of the Canton area of South China. It cannot be known whether the inhabitants of that region were in some contact by sea with western Asia before they were incorporated in the Han Empire, for they had no written records. Late in the Han Empire, in A.D. 166, an embassy from An Tun King of Ta Ts'in (the Emperor Marcus Aurelius Antoninus) is recorded by the Chinese as having reached the Court, coming by sea. The Chinese suspected that the 'ambassadors' were really merchants assuming this high title, because their presents were not Roman products, but objects obtained in south-east Asia. The fact, however, together with some archaeological finds of Roman objects in Thailand and elsewhere proves that a trade route did already exist, via the Red Sea, Ceylon, Siam, Malaya, and the Vietnam coast. A second embassy, apparently more official in character, arrived in China shortly after the fall of the Han dynasty. Later the route was used by Buddhist pilgrims and missionaries passing to and from India. But as a means of close connexion with the Roman world it was hardly as significant as the land route across Central Asia.

Buddhism, Confucianism, and Taoism

The most significant, and the most enduring, result of these new contacts was the discovery of India, and the subsequent introduction of Buddhism to China and the Far East, mainly by the land route to the north-west. Buddhism was until modern times the major, almost the only strong foreign influence affecting the Chinese culture, and the only one which left a permanent mark. The influence of Buddhism on art and on religious thought was great and lasting, but it had little effect on the social or political outlook of the Chinese, and the contact with India remained slight, confined to religion and a little trade, without political importance.

The spread of Buddhism in China after the end of the Han dynasty has been compared with the conversion of the Roman Empire to Christianity. In both cases the new, universal, religion was of foreign origin: in both cases the opposition was on the one hand ethical philosophic systems only tenuously related to the old popular religion, on the other diverse and traditional polytheism. But here the similarities end. Buddhism was transmitted to China by Indian monks bringing with them their Sanskrit sacred

texts. The Chinese at that period had little experience of
foreign languages of a widely different grammatical structure and were unacquainted with any system of writing
except their own. The work of translation was thus difficult and slow. Several centuries passed before the major
corpus of Buddhist scripture was fully translated, and the
necessity to use Chinese ideographs made this at best an
approximate rendering in which names were greatly dis-
torted. India was far away, communications were slow
and hard, very few men ever made more than one journey
to the sacred land and thence returned to China. In India
itself Buddhism was already on the decline.

The new creed was thus only slenderly supported by a
body of foreign knowledge, of which very few scholars had
any mastery. The source of inspiration was remote, the
contact slight and intermittent, no political power of any
importance to China stood behind Buddhism in its home-
land. The introduction of Buddhism had more the character of a transplantation and acclimatization than of a conversion. The Indian view of the universe, as expressed in
Buddhist teaching, made only a limited impression, which
did not succeed in effacing the long established Chinese
cosmology. Men believed, as Buddhists, in the transmigra-
tion of souls and the progress through enlightenment to
Nirvana. At the same time, as Confucians, the educated
firmly supported the rites of ancestor worship, the traditional beliefs associated with those rites, and the claims
of the Emperor to be the mediating priest between Heaven
and Earth. The population, as they still do, adopted
Buddhist saints and made them into local gods on the
same footing as those they already worshipped. These in-
consistencies did not (and do not) trouble the Chinese
mind. Confucian teaching was never driven from the
schools, and remained the governing ethic. Taoism, gather-
ing to itself the incoherent polytheism of the earlier age,

B

maintained a steady rivalry. There was thus no true Buddhist conquest of the Chinese world; Buddhism infiltrated, won itself a respected and abiding place, but was kept to that place, and it was not the seat of government or the schoolroom.

Buddhism also never escaped the reproach of being a foreign creed. Confucian scholars of all subsequent ages continued to make this charge, and to draw the conclusion that to believe in the Buddha meant to ignore the teaching of the Sage (Confucius) and thus to deny the real basis of morality. They objected, specifically, to Buddhist celibacy as contrary to the duty of filial piety, since man should provide posterity to revere the ancestors. They objected on more philosophic grounds to the doctrine of Karma, since if man's condition was the result of sin or virtue in a former incarnation, the actual individual now living was not indebted to his ancestors for his prosperity nor restrained from vice by considering the prospective misery of his posterity. In the early centuries of Buddhist evangelism, when the tide seemed to be running very strongly in favour of the new religion, there were brief Confucian- or Taoist-inspired persecutions of the Buddhists, often taking the form of the compulsory marriage of monks and nuns, only rarely proceeding to martyrdoms.

Buddhism had indeed received strong support from the alien nomadic conqerors who had overrun the north of China about a century after the fall of the Han dynasty (A.D. 316). It is clear from the early works of art in the great Buddhist shrine at Yun Kang in north Shansi that in the fifth century many of the craftsmen there employed were not Chinese, and hardly a Chinese inscription appears in the earliest parts of the cave-temple complex. Indian and also Hellenistic motifs abound. Buddhism was accepted in the southern, Chinese, Empire, but there seems no doubt that in the early ages it was stronger in the north, and under the direct patronage of the alien rulers, who were naturally not at first trained to be Confucian scholars. The need which these foreign conquerors had to use the Chinese scholar gentry to administer their kingdoms, the small numbers of the conquering tribes, the already very large Chinese population, resulted in a rapid swamping of the nomadic element and its way of life. Within a generation or two they lost their language, learned to read and write Chinese, became, at least to some degree, Confucians, and intermarried with the native Chinese.

The possiblity that this invasion of foreign peoples, supporting a new religion, would effect a permanent mutation of the Chinese culture, as the barbarian invasions and Christianity combined did to the Roman-Greek civilization of Europe, thus disappeared. When China was reunited and consolidated in a new centralized empire under the T'ang dynasty in the early seventh century, it was essentially the culture of the old empire which was revived and fortified. Buddhism remained, but other alien influences brought in by the foreign conquerors of North China faded out. From the T'ang period onward the Chinese state remained far more often united under one dynasty than divided between two or more: the ideals of the unified empire came to be regarded as normal and right, and these ideals were based upon the traditional Chinese concepts, which made the empire the synonym of the civilized world, treating all beyond China as barbarian.

Since this turning-point, at which the Chinese world outlook became so firmly established that it has never subsequently altered until modern times, is clearly of fundamental importance, it is necessary to consider what were the reasons which made it possible for China to be reunited, and to remain so; to reject one strong alien influence, to absorb another, and to establish a political system which, though often shaken, was always restored.

Partial foreign conquest

There were several important respects in which the situation of China in the age of partial foreign conquest from A.D. 316 to 589 differed from that of the period of the barbarian invasions of the Roman Empire, with which it was roughly contemporary. There was in China no 'Dark Age'. At no time did the literature of the past become scarce, books cease to be written, history pass unrecorded. Even in the alien-conquered north this was true. The Chinese soon taught the barbarians to read, they did not forget the art themselves. Language was not transformed so that the old classical language became 'dead' except to a small educated minority. The Chinese language continued to be spoken, and written, in north and south alike: it was the foreign tongues which quickly disappeared, leaving, it would seem, very few traces, even in personal names. There was thus a firm basis on which old traditions could be sustained and old practices revived.

These conditions were assured by two other factors: the demographic strength of the Chinese population and the geographical contiguity of the two halves of the country. There is adequate contemporary evidence to show that the nomad invaders were a small minority of the population and that the Chinese population was already very large. There were probably not less than thirty to forty million Chinese in the conquered area, and hardly one million of the nomadic conquerors. They had seized the country in swift campaigns during an age of confusion and weakness. They held control by relying on their military power at first, and on the co-operation of the Chinese landowning class thereafter. To obtain this co-operation they had to share their power, encourage the arts favoured by the Chinese, accept their ideas, and revere their beliefs. The cultural unity of the Chinese world was thus very slightly impaired by the conquest. This was in part also due to geographical factors. Unlike the Roman Empire, the Chinese Empire was not bilingual. There was nothing to correspond with the Greek-speaking East and the Latin-speaking West. The southern half of the Chinese Empire, which remained under Chinese rule, spoke the same language (possibly with more variety of dialects) and also wrote the same language as the northern half which had been conquered.

Very many of the great families of the north, with their retainers and followers, moved to the south and established themselves in the new lands beyond the Yangtze. They brought with them the culture of the old centre of Chinese civilization and established it in the south, which had been a backward, provincial region under the Han. But this region, although differing in climate and produce from the north, is none the less adjacent to it, on a long land border, mainly without important natural obstacles. Mountain chains, neither very high nor impassable, separate the basins of the Yangtze and Yellow Rivers in the western section, but farther east the two regions merge in an indeterminate border—open, mainly plain and marsh, offering little obstacle to the passage of men or armies. No line could then be drawn, or ever has been drawn, which clearly demarcates North from South China. The Yangtze was the artery of the Southern Empire, but not its frontier, which lay northward along the low ranges or in the complex waterways of the Huai valley. The frontier fluctuated with the fortunes of an almost constant warfare. The geographical basis for a lasting division of the empire was lacking. In the former Roman world the differences of race, language, and later of religion reinforced a separation which the Adriatic already imposed: in China an identity of race, language, and tradition reinforced a unity which geography required.

The most populous and most sophisticated region of the Roman world was the east, the lands of ancient civilization, Syria, Asia Minor, Greece, and Egypt. It was this area which was retained by the Byzantine monarchs; the original Roman west was overrun by the barbarians. Gaul, Spain, and Britain had not been the centres of ancient cultures, they had until Roman conquest been barbarian. In China it was the northern lands, the ancient centre of Chinese civilization, which were seized by the Tatar invaders. The colonial south, then very thinly settled, mainly in the Yangtze valley, was saved for the Chinese more by the difficulty of the terrain and by maritime power operating on the great river than by the prowess of armies in the field. The European invaders were able to maintain themselves in a region which had only a few generations earlier been inhabited by communities much like themselves; the Tatar invaders found themselves in a country densely inhabited by a civilized people, studded with cities. The barbarians in the West assimilated the Roman provincials, the barbarians of North China were assimilated by the Chinese majority.

The north remained, in that age, still far more populous; the south retained the tradition of the unified empire, claimed to be its inheritor, never acknowledged the validity of the partition. All that was needed to effect reunion was the relatively complete absorption of the nomadic military caste into the main body of the northern Chinese landowning aristocracy, and this had been effected by intermarriage by the end of the sixth century. When a Chinese leader from the north, a member of this aristocracy of mixed descent, seized the northern throne (from his Tatar father-in-law), his easy conquest of the south was accepted without any of the strong resistance which the south had put up against earlier attempts by rulers of pure Tatar blood. If Charlemagne had been half-Greek with a Byzantine education, and could have marched his armies from Italy to Greece without crossing the sea, something of the same sort might conceivably have happened in Europe. But Sui Kao Tsu, who first reunited China, also ruled over the most populous part of the empire before he conquered the south.

2

The Golden Age of the T'ang Empire

Reunification

IT is significant that in the succeeding period, that of the T'ang dynasty, which ruled for 300 years (A.D. 618–907), no serious rebellion arose in the south. There was never any attempt to shake off the rule of the dynasty, although it reigned in a northern capital. There were never again, indeed, any movements which sought to divide the empire in favour of local régimes based on the defined regions of south, west, or north. Rebellions were frequent, but the purpose of the rebel leaders was to make themselves emperors of all China. If they failed to do so, they were defeated and destroyed. Briefly, at the collapse of the T'ang in the early tenth century China was divided between several aspirant emperors, for fifty years, until one arose strong enough to conquer all the others. In later ages a renewed foreign invasion of the Kin Tatars wrested the north from the Sung, but failed to conquer the south to which the Sung dynasty retired. The Mongols conquered both, and reunited China. The Ming ousted the Mongols and restored Chinese rule throughout the even larger empire. Unity became the norm, division only the result of confusion, or partial, passing, foreign conquests.

Under the T'ang dynasty the penetration of the south continued until all of the modern territory of the Chinese state had been colonized and absorbed into the empire except the present extreme south-west mountain region, the province of Yunnan. That area was finally incorporated by the Mongols and the Ming. These advances brought the Chinese to the limit of the region which suited their way of life. Chinese civilization, and for a time, rule, spread down the coast of Vietnam, but it was later found better to leave this outpost as a tributary kingdom rather than hold it as a province. The same sequence occurred in Korea, conquered by the T'ang, but later left to rule itself under Chinese suzerainty. Further advances, under the Manchu dynasty, were of the nature of imperialist conquest of border peoples, but not an expansion of China proper.

Rather more than 1,000 years ago the T'ang dynasty thus fixed the geographical limits in which the Chinese people were to live until modern times. There was little incentive to go beyond them: the population, known from the careful census-taking of the dynasty, did not then exceed 60 millions, allowing for the fact that the highest figure recorded may have omitted a large number (52,880,488). This population occupied an area comparable to the territory of the modern republic less the provinces of Yunnan and part of Kueichou, but including most of the southern half of Manchuria and also the Tongking area of north Vietnam. The present population of the equivalent regions would exceed 500 millions. For those who found the old northern provinces already too crowded, there was ample new land to be found in the south, and the flow of migrants into South China was continuous. The T'ang emperors had no reason to conquer distant lands, and apart from extending their authority over the old trade route to west Asia across Sinkiang, they did not do so.

Contacts with foreigners

Trade with distant countries was growing in importance. Japan, which had now emerged as a coherent state, although soon to be divided between feudal lords, was eagerly borrowing the arts and sciences of China. The Arabs had developed the sea route from the Red Sea, and formed large trading communities in the southern ports. The route across Central Asia kept T'ang China in constant touch with India and Persia, and in more sporadic communication with Byzantium. All these countries were known to the Chinese, and are described by them in the dynastic history and other contemporary works. Foreigners and some foreign ways were well known to the population of the capital and great cities. The T'ang official class employed Indian jugglers, West Asian grooms, possibly had some Negro servants (from east Africa), and many other nationalities are portrayed in the pottery grave figures which were buried in the tombs of the wealthy.

Yet there is little doubt that the T'ang Chinese received nothing from these contacts with foreigners which shook their conviction of their own superiority. The foreign residents, servants, merchants, and pilgrims served a useful purpose, but they certainly held no position of equality. Following the fall of the Persian empire of the Sasanids, in the early seventh century, many Persian refugees came to China, including the last king, Yesdegerd. They sought to gain the support of China for the recovery of Persia from the Arab conquerors, but such assistance as they received was slight and their efforts abortive. Later the son and grandson of Yesdegerd served in the T'ang army, and the family no doubt merged gradually with the Chinese aristocracy of the time. It is probable that there were many other refugees, less distinguished in ancestry, who had a similar fortune. These Persians and religious teachers, Buddhist and Nestorian, seem to be the only element among the foreign population which stood at a higher level of education than the pedlars, grooms, jugglers, and other entertainers who are so plentifully represented among the tomb figures.

There was for many years an easy toleration of foreign religions, introduced by such visitors, and mainly serving their communities. Persian Zoroastrians had their temple in Ch'angan, the capital. The Nestorians, who came from the eastern provinces of the Byzantine empire, built their church and recorded the story of their mission on a famous, still surviving stone tablet. They seem to have spread into the provinces, at least to large cities, but it has never been clear whether their congregations included many Chinese, or were mostly traders from the Levant. In the capital they enjoyed the favour of the Court and may have had some influence on the ruling class. Manichæans, also of Persian origin, enjoyed some success in the later T'ang period, mainly among the foreign mercenaries from Central Asia serving in the T'ang forces. It was in this same way that Islam was first introduced to China, at least in the north-western provinces, although there is evidence that Arab merchants brought it to Canton by sea at much the same period. The two oldest mosques in China, respectively in Ch'angan and Canton, date from the T'ang period.

It is therefore certain that in T'ang China there was a much wider contact with the west Asian and even Eastern European (Byzantine) world than had ever occurred before, or was to recur until modern times, with the exception of the relatively short period of Mongol conquest (thirteenth century). Yet there was little in these contacts to make a deep impression upon the Chinese outlook or shake the established conceptions of China's place in the world. It was indeed, to the Chinese of that time, obvious that they lived in the most advanced community of which they had knowledge, and the further contacts with distant states confirmed them in this belief.

It was true: the seventh, eighth, and ninth centuries A.D. are not a period which the Western world would claim as among the peaks of its civilization. Most of Europe was by the end of this epoch just emerging from the Dark Ages. Byzantium alone upheld the civilization of the past. It was Byzantium with which the Chinese had some contact, sufficient for them to recognize the Eastern Empire as the heir and continuer of that earlier empire they had called Ta Ts'in; sufficient, perhaps, to know that the heir was only possessed of a fraction of the old estate. Their records and comments, which include a good description of Constantinople, are not derogatory, but they lack that quality of wonder and admiration which Han accounts of the Roman Empire certainly show. India was the Holy Land of Buddhism: or rather it had been the Land of Buddha. By T'ang times Buddhist shrines in India were falling into neglect; the north-western region of the sub-continent, now fanatically Moslem, was then the last centre of active Buddhism, and was soon to be overwhelmed by Moslem conquest. In the T'ang period the pilgrims who went to India were conscious of this falling off and anxious to collect scriptures and relics while there was yet time. India, in any case, was politically incoherent, and contained no organized large state in any way comparable with China.

The T'ang Chinese had probably more knowledge of, and perhaps respect for, Persia, until the Arab conquest overthrew it. The tradition that the poet Li Po could speak Persian is a rare instance of any record that a Chinese scholar was acquainted with (or interested in) a foreign language or culture, the Buddhist Sanskrit scholars being the exception. How far this interest in Persia was a consequence of the presence in and about Court of important Persian refugees (as seems probable) is not on record.

The barbarism of other peoples

The knowledge of these far-off civilized countries and their troubles enhanced by contrast the splendour of the

T'ang empire. It was far larger than any competitor, however distant. It was richer; its arts, sciences, and literature were more varied and developed. It was certainly better governed, with a degree of administrative efficiency which was not equalled anywhere else until the eighteenth century. Records of this administration, preserved in the dynastic history, stand to prove that until the empire was weakened by rebellions and military usurpations in its later years it was ruled by a well-trained, highly educated civil service, now recruited by public examinations. No other state evolved these techniques of modern government till more than 1,000 years later.

The experience of the T'ang thus powerfully reinforced the Chinese belief in their own superiority, and in the relative—or absolute—barbarism of other peoples. With the exception of the distant countries of western Asia, mainly known through their merchants, the only civilized peoples were those such as the Koreans and Japanese who had adopted Chinese culture and remodelled their own institutions in the image of China. The foreigners best known to the Chinese were the nomads of the Mongolian Steppe, at this period the Turks (who had not yet migrated westward).

Frontier policy, designed to keep these barbarians out of China and under control of the Court, resulted in a long series of border wars, which from the Chinese point of view were successful. Incursions of a serious character were few and never achieved any lasting conquest. The T'ang army, principally made up of heavy armed cavalry, backed by the garrisons of the passes through the Great Wall, was a highly trained force, recruited on a regular basis partly from 'friendly' tribes, partly from soldier-settler colonies who held their lands within the Wall on condition of military service. It therefore became a professional army, more and more divorced from the old aristocracy which at the beginning of the dynasty had served equally in the army and in civil administration. This situation later involved the dynasty in disasters, but it remains an early example of a 'modern' style army, very different from the mercenary bands and feudal levies of the Byzantine Empire or the emerging kingdoms of Europe.

In order to get the perspective of the Chinese outlook it is necessary to stress the achievements of the T'ang period, remote though it seems to the modern age, because this dynasty set the model which the Chinese strove to restore or to imitate as long as the empire lasted. The institutions of the later empire with rare exceptions took their origin in the practices or innovations of the T'ang period. The key organization of the government, the civil service recruited by public examination (which the West borrowed from China centuries later), was essentially a T'ang invention. Previous to that period officials were advanced and recommended by sponsors, were in fact 'placemen' in the seventeenth-century English sense of the term. They belonged, therefore, to families who were clients of great men, and the aristocratic domination of the government was thus perpetuated. The T'ang system, consciously designed to reduce the too great power of this aristocracy, successfully replaced it by a civil service recruited from a far wider class of literate gentry. There can be little doubt that the stability of later dynasties, and the long continuance of the Chinese Empire in spite of changes of dynasties, were fundamentally due to this institution, which all later régimes cherished and restored.

In Confucian theory, to which all paid lip-service, the Golden Age lay in the remote past, and all that had followed was but decline or feeble imitation. Practical men in later Chinese history saw the T'ang as the effective 'golden age' whose acts and institutions were well recorded and could be imitated. 'Rule like the T'ang' was the claim and injunction to his successors inscribed on the tomb of the founder of the Ming dynasty, himself a man of the humblest origin, and long illiterate. In the periods which followed the T'ang, foreign pressures from better organized nomadic peoples weighed heavily on China. The Sung never controlled the full length of the northern frontier, and were thus open to constant attack, which finally overcame them. The Mongol conquest, although it lasted a bare century over all China, was a violent breach in the T'ang tradition. The examinations were discontinued, foreigners were employed as civil servants, the very Chinese language was hardly used at Court. Against this the Chinese reaction was eventually wholly triumphant. The Ming expelled the Mongols and endeavoured to restore 'T'ang rule'. Whether they fully achieved this objective may be disputed, but they certainly restored the T'ang tradition.

The Manchus, a people who had already had two generations of strong Chinese cultural influence before they entered China and established their dynasty, were very careful to flatter the Chinese by upholding the T'ang tradition in every way open to them. Ch'ien Lung, one of their greatest rulers, liked nothing better than to be compared with T'ang T'ai Tsung, the true founder of the T'ang. The state of the world and the position of China in it had in reality changed profoundly in the thousand years since the foundation of the T'ang, but the Manchu rulers were unable and unwilling to recognize this truth. So long as they tried to 'rule like the T'ang' China would accept them, aliens though they might be in origin. To innovate, to use foreign ways and foreign inventions would be to incur the danger to which the Mongols had succumbed, to provoke a furious reaction from the Chinese, determined, like the Ming, to restore the rule of T'ang. The traditions of the great dynasty had been an inspiration: they were now to become a drug.

But nothing which had happened to China during that long period had sufficed to convince the Chinese that their ancient model and accepted outlook were inadequate. The foreign conquerors they had repelled or endured had been peoples of less advanced culture, contributing little or nothing of value to the Chinese civilization. They were 'barbarians': therefore all foreigners who came in arms were also barbarians. The Mongols had been superior in military matters, but in these alone: the evident superiority of the Europeans in this respect, therefore, did not impress the Chinese as proof of cultural equality, but rather tended to show them in an unfavourable light.

3

China and the Modern World

The Chinese and Christianity

THE early Western visitors were of a character which confirmed the Chinese view of them as 'barbarians'. To the sixteenth-century Portuguese China was certainly the farthest possible port of call. It was necessary to round the Cape of Good Hope, cross the Indian Ocean, and continue the long voyage through the Straits of Malacca and the South China Sea, the haunts of Malay pirates. Only the hope of great profit and the courage of reckless adventurers could induce men to undertake voyages on which the prospect of safe return was at best fifty-fifty. It was, consequently, not the most learned, cultivated, and mature element in Western civilization which the Chinese first encountered. Even the missionaries did not begin to arrive along the coasts of China until several decades after the traders, who had already established a reputation for unruly violence which was well deserved. It is an interesting fact that although the presence of large colonies of Arab traders in the T'ang and Sung dynasties is attested in Chinese records of the southern ports, it is never recorded that these foreign merchants caused troubles and resorted to arms. On the other hand, the Portuguese did so from their first contacts. A possible explanation is the differing traditions of the two peoples: the Arabs had traded among 'infidels' for many centuries, and learned to curb their religious zeal. The Portuguese brought with them to the eastern seas the fierce antipathies of the Barbary Coast, the militant outlook of the Iberian Crusades.

There was, therefore, little in the conduct of the new-comers from the West, or in their character either, which could induce the Chinese to alter their belief that these foreigners from across the sea were as barbarous as those known to them by the land routes. It was the hope of the more educated among the Western voyagers that the violence and cupidity of the sailors and merchants could be offset by the piety, humility, and single-minded devotion of the missionary monks who soon began to accompany the traders to the East. They would show the pagan Chinese that Europe also possessed a great culture, based, moreover, on true religion, and thus in every essential superior to that of the East, however refined this might be in some respects. The prospect seemed fair; the missionaries soon discovered that China had no single, monolithic, hostile religion such as Islam. In many ways the scholars among the missionaries saw China as in a similar situation to the Roman world in the last age of paganism. They remembered that the conversion of the empire had been finally effected by converting the Emperor. What was needed was a Chinese Constantine.

The first Portuguese ships to reach China had touched at Canton in 1516. It was not until nearly sixty years later that the first missionaries were permitted to land in Canton, but in little more than twenty years after that (1598) Father Matteo Ricci had established himself in Peking and begun the great attempt to convert China from the top. This effort, sustained for the whole of the seventeenth century, brought the Chinese educated class, for the first time for centuries, into some contact with foreigners of education and deep learning. The Jesuit missionaries were scholars of great distinction. Proficient in the languages and sciences of the West, they also studied and mastered the Chinese classics, learned to speak and to write Chinese, translated the Bible into Chinese, and also rendered

Chinese classical and historical works into Latin, and later, French. Their knowledge of mathematics and astronomy was in advance of that of China, and their corrections to the calendar, their ability to make accurate predictions concerning eclipses, were highly appreciated at Court. It might have seemed as if a new and powerful cultural influence was about to enter China, which would lead to wide revisions in the Chinese outlook.

Ultimately, in other ways, the contact with the West did have this effect: but the reaction was long delayed and when it came repudiated the religion which the West had offered as the finest fruit of its civilization. The attempt to convert China from the top failed: so did later attempts to convert the Chinese people themselves. There were factors in the situation which the early missionaries could not be expected to perceive, and which their later successors did not, perhaps, want to acknowledge. Trained in the European tradition, and soaked in its history both theological and lay, the missionaries could not realize that some of the assumptions of their own culture were simply lacking to the Chinese. The Westerners saw religion as revealed truth, battling with infidelity, heresy, and 'false gods'. It had been so for 2,000 years: since the persecutions of the early Church, through the conversion of the pagans, the struggle with Islam, the conflicts of the Reformation. There could be no compromise: there was Truth and Error.

These ideas were unfamiliar to the Chinese. They had no one revealed religious truth: there was Buddhism, but also Confucianism, and moreover Taoism. Three Ways, as they were called. No one suggested that the 'ways', or two of them, were blind alleys. On the contrary, the Three Ways led to One Goal. The Goal was not Heaven, or salvation, but the righteous life on earth. Unpreoccupied by the search for the ultimate explanation, the Chinese had always directed their thoughts to the ordering of human relationships. The doctrines of Confucius and of his later followers are concentrated on a social, almost a political message. The Sage himself considered that the needs of men were his concern, and that the worship of the gods need not be the subject of any inquiry. Later writers in the Sung period found it necessary to pay more attention to the wider questions of philosophy, if only to counter the teaching of Buddhism. But they too repudiated deism even more decisively than Confucius himself. They saw the universe as governed by moral law, but to this force they specifically denied personality. The conception of the jealous God, the exclusive truth, was unknown to them.

Buddhism taught that man, through many transmigrations and reincarnations, might, by acquiring knowledge, rise above the illusions of existence and enter the state of Nirvana, the absence of striving. This can hardly be equated with the idea of personal salvation, since the process of achieving unity with the Buddha is of vast duration, in many lives, and the ultimate goal is personal annihilation, or total submergence in the primal unity. Taoism, the popular polytheism which that ancient quietist philosophy had now become, was ready enough to add another god to its comprehensive pantheon, but saw no reason, on that account, to exclude those already there. It was the very fact that the Chinese had no overriding religion, no one doctrine, that defeated the missionary enterprise. The attempt, in this late age, to introduce a wholly new conception running counter to the long established traditions of the Chinese civilization, could not succeed unless those traditions and the civilization they had fostered were overthrown and utterly destroyed. Before many years had passed the Chinese came to understand that this was what was really involved. The missionaries were not ready to accept so hard a conclusion, but in the nineteenth century the Protestant missionaries came generally to a tacit realization of this truth.

There were other, lesser, obstacles. The Christian religion in all its forms was foreign. To the Chinese this was already a serious failing, and one which Buddhism, after nearly 2,000 years, had not by any means overcome. To accept a foreign teaching implied that the wisdom of China was deficient, and that the foreigner, barbarian though he was, had something better to offer. This was to the Chinese a contradiction in terms. China was civilization, always had been, could not now be thrust down from this supreme position. The foreigners, even if some of them had curious skills and valuable knowledge in a limited field, were still members of distant barbarian peoples, who could not be expected to be the equals of Chinese in any respect. Moreover the educated Chinese, since the Sung interpretations of Confucian doctrine had become orthodox, no longer had any faith in the supernatural, and regarded such beliefs as rustic, unsophisticated, uneducated. They were thus quite unwilling to give serious consideration to a doctrine which was based upon the belief in the supernatural and derived all its theology and ethic from the commandments of God.

Superstition was accepted as natural to the common people, to be tolerated, humoured, even patronized, so long as it kept the people contented, obedient to their rulers, and faithful to the governing ethic of Confucian doctrine. But all creeds which stirred up popular excitement, appealed to mass emotions, repudiated the existing authority and called in question the orthodoxy of Confucian teaching were to be firmly and ruthlessly suppressed. Before many years had gone by the scholar gentry more and more formed the conclusion that Christianity came into this class and was a social menace. Missionary enterprise was hindered, then forbidden.

So long as the Manchu dynasty, in this faithfully reflecting the prevalent opinions of the Chinese educated class, was strong enough to exclude Christian teaching and limit the activity of the few Catholic missionaries to strictly supervised scientific work, the contact with the West remained slight. Trade might enrich the merchants of Canton, but it was carried on under rigid rules causing great inconvenience to the foreign merchant. Up to the end of the eighteenth century the Chinese world still stood intact, aloof, uninterested in the West, unwilling to learn, unable to believe that the barbarians had anything of value to communicate. The Emperor Ch'ien Lung, refusing the request of George III's ambassador for permanent diplomatic and easier trade relations, typified, in a famous edict, the unchanged outlook of his many predecessors, who in their time, had better reasons for believing in their own superiority.

As to what you have requested in your message, O King, namely to be allowed to send one of your subjects to reside in the Celestial Empire to look after your Country's trade, this does not conform to the Celestial Empire's ceremonial system, and definitely cannot be done. . . . The Celestial Empire, ruling all within the four seas . . . does not value rare and precious things. . . . We have never valued ingenious articles, nor do we have the slightest need of your Country's manufactures.[1]

The Western view of nineteenth-century China

In the nineteenth century all this was changed. There is perhaps no greater example of a reversal of opinions than the contrast between the early Jesuit assessment of the Chinese Empire, made in the beginning of the eighteenth century, and the views which became universal among

[1] J. L. Cranmer-Byng, 'Lord Macartney's Embassy to Peking in 1793, from Official Chinese Documents', *Journal of Oriental Studies*, iv (1957–8), 134–7.

Europeans by the end of the nineteenth. To the first missionaries, and to their immediate successors, China was a magnificent spectacle: an empire far larger than any Europe had known since the fall of Rome, governed by a central administration through officers appointed, removed, transferred, or dismissed at the pleasure of the Throne, unhampered by feudal privileges or local powers. It possessed a vast historical record far more accurate, better dated, and reaching back farther than any comparable achievement of the West. Commerce passed unrestricted over the huge territories of the Ch'ing dynasty. In arts and learning the Chinese at least equalled anything known to Europe. In one respect alone the Chinese were deficient. They were not Christians. The early European visitors did not pay much regard to those matters which later historians may well consider more important defects in the Chinese polity. Poverty then, as ever, stood in naked contrast to the great luxury of the Court and official class. Disease flourished; famine, in bad years, was frequent; floods and other natural disasters could not be palliated owing to the lack of effective communications.

But all these ills afflicted eighteenth-century Europe hardly less. France and Spain, Italy and Portugal, whence the missionaries came, showed the same contrast between wealth and poverty, were equally plagued by epidemics for which science yet knew no remedy, suffered from famines and from other disasters, had poor roads and corrupt government. The missionaries were well accustomed to see these things as the consequences of the Fall of Man, an inevitable condition of life on earth, which rulers might try to relieve, but could not be expected to remove. Perhaps because they passed their lives far from home and were in any case unacquainted with those parts of Europe where new and pregnant developments were beginning to take shape, the missionaries presented Europe with an idyllic picture of China, which was eagerly accepted by those philosophers who were most ready to criticize the ancient institutions of their own countries.

By the middle of the nineteenth century totally different views prevailed. China was weak, corrupt, ill-governed, racked by rebellions, swept by famine, ignorant of science, indifferent to progress, and still pagan. Some things had indeed changed, on both sides. The Manchu dynasty declined rapidly after the death of Ch'ien Lung, for causes which were not wholly due to the failing abilities of the sovereigns, but were in part the result of the long peace established by the earlier great rulers. In this period of over a century the population had very rapidly increased, the area of free land had not been extended, and the consequent misery caused by crop failures, floods, and droughts was felt more widely and by many more people. K'ang Hsi and Ch'ien Lung had ended the nomad menace on the northern frontier, by the conquest of Mongolia. The result was that the military power of the state was allowed to decline, since the constant incentive of the northern border war was now removed. No attempt was made to keep pace with the advancing techniques of the West, developed as they had been by a long period of large-scale warfare. When the British went to war with China in 1839–42 it was found that the giant had feet of clay, the Manchu forces were medieval in equipment, no match for small numbers of European troops. This was made clearer still when the British and French in 1860 took Peking itself and forced the Emperor into flight.

It is a regrettable fact that the value of a nation's contribution to civilization, her place in the world, tends to be judged, from age to age, by the strength or weakness of her military power. When China under K'ang Hsi or Ch'ien Lung was manifestly too strong for any European encroachment to succeed, the real and serious weaknesses of the government and economy were not regarded; the achievements in art and literature were much respected. When China fell behind Europe, her military power becoming negligible, encroachment was continual, and the value of Chinese civilization fell sharply in Western eyes. Poverty and disease, now somewhat abated in Europe, were decried in China, art and literature, which had changed very little, were no longer admired or imitated. The pre-industrial outlook which all peoples had held in common a century before was now attributed to China as a local and peculiar failing of her people. The Europeans were more than ever convinced that China's only hope was in her conversion to Christianity and the adoption of the civilization of the West.

But the Chinese, both rulers and people, were by no means convinced of this. They held on the contrary to the view that as the barbarians were proving more dangerous than they had seemed to be at first, it was the more necessary to keep them out of China, and reduce contacts with them. Forced by defeat in war to admit the trader to more ports, to permit the missionary, Protestant now as well as Catholic, to preach at will throughout the land, the government continued to obstruct, delay, and when possible frustrate the provisions of the treaties. The people developed a dangerous xenophobia which broke out from time to time in riots, murders, and massacres. The Chinese government seemed to have reason on its side. The T'ai P'ing rebellion, which shook the dynasty in the mid-nineteenth century, was led by men strongly influenced by Christian teaching, men who believed themselves prophets of a new faith; they burnt Buddhist and Taoist temples, persecuted Confucian scholars, and showed no respect to the Sage. It was, therefore, obvious that here were the fruits of missionary endeavour.

Missionaries were under the protection of foreign powers:

if they suffered injury the powers demanded reparation from the Chinese government, often far in excess of just compensation. The maltreatment or murder of missionaries were made the pretext for territorial and political exactions. As it was the xenophobia of the people, not the acts of the officials, which brought about these incidents, the government was placed in a humiliating position. By accepting the demands of the foreign powers they 'lost face' in the eyes of the people; the officials who were dismissed for failing to protect a missionary, whose activities they disliked as much as did the populace that had injured him, were shown up as impotent, helpless victims of foreign pressure.

Conservatives and reformers

The reaction which these pressures produced was not to make the Chinese feel that there must be great merits, hitherto unsuspected, in the civilization of Europe. Two schools of thought formed. There were those who believed that a great effort should be made to strengthen the dynasty, recover the ancient power, and use it to expel the foreigner root and branch. Since all the foreigner brought was in their eyes evil—and in the case of opium they had a glaring example—nothing foreign could be used, or should be accepted. The old ways of China, tried and trusted for so many centuries, should suffice, provided they were directed by men of true Confucian training and pure principles.

Another school saw that to rely on the outmoded methods and weapons of an earlier age was hopeless. The foreigner, they admitted, had one valuable technique: his knowledge of how to make modern weapons. They did not reflect that this knowledge was an outgrowth of a wider technology, many manifestations of which remained unknown to them. They took no interest in what the foreigner could do in the realm of industry and pure science. But the weapons were needed. Under the guidance of these men, whom the age regarded as reformers, even modernizers, arsenals were built, modern warships constructed, and troops trained in Western methods and armed with rifles and artillery. But most of these reformers set their faces against the building of railways, which would only make foreign invasions more easy. They opposed mining enterprises because they saw no value in industrial development. They accepted steamers reluctantly, because of their evident value for moving troops on the great rivers of China.

Those who wished to 'use foreign ways to protect Chinese ideas' ultimately won the struggle. By slow degrees the type of modernization they admitted gained entrance to China: railways were built and mining was developed, but one consequence of the reluctance of the Chinese educated class to adopt modern technology was that this retarded development fell almost completely into foreign hands, thus actually increasing, not diminishing, the dependence of China on foreign power. The exponents of the other doctrine, perhaps vaguely aware of this, became more chauvinistic than before, and this culminated in the support given by the Court, under the influence of this party, to the Boxer Movement, a violent peasant uprising not only aimed at eliminating the foreigner but also directed against all Chinese under any foreign influence, however slight. Christian converts, people who wore articles of Western attire or even articles of Western manufacture, who used implements of European make, all were to be destroyed. The Movement was crushed by the international expedition of the Western powers, and with it fell the prestige of the Court. Only a short interval now remained before revolution overthrew the age-old institutions of China.

Intellectuals and Western culture

During the last years of the nineteenth century a new outlook had rapidly made way among the younger Chinese intellectuals. Convinced of the futility of the 'ultra' party and their hope of expelling the foreigner, convinced, too, that the cautious modernizers were going too slowly, and could not in reality protect Chinese civilization by using Western technology, they now believed that a much more drastic change was essential. China must give up much that she had always cherished, including her belief in her traditional form of government. An attempt was made to use the Throne in the manner of the Meiji Restoration in Japan to sanction and direct a programme of sweeping reforms (1898). This was frustrated by the reactionary party, and thenceforward the advanced reformers, abandoning any hope of support from the dynasty, campaigned for a revolution and a republic.

The rapidity and the thoroughness of the change in outlook which then took place in the Chinese educated class is a phenomenon which deserves more attention than it often receives. Shortly after the Boxer Movement had been crushed, and already some years earlier than that, the great majority of the younger generation of Chinese scholar gentry had become revolutionary in outlook, some willing to go farther than others, but all eager to 'drink foreign ink'—to learn Western knowledge, to study abroad, acquire the secret of Western power. Only a generation earlier the fathers of these men had mostly opposed any admission of foreign learning, had derided the knowledge of the West, had harried the missionary, held off the trader, and, even when personally more friendly to individual foreigners, remained in profound ignorance of Europe, its civilization and its thought.

The father of an eminent Chinese of our own time was

astonished, when conversing with a missionary doctor with whom he was friendly, to learn by chance that England produced poetry as well as guns, and had a wide literature and a deep scholarship. He was himself a high official of the empire and an accomplished scholar. In 1870 only a tiny handful of Chinese knew any European language (except the 'pidgin' of the merchants). By 1910 at the latest English was the second language of the schools, and very many more Chinese could read and speak it than there were Europeans who could speak (let alone read) Chinese. The Old China Hand of the early twentieth century was content to pass thirty years in China without learning a word of the language.

But this surge for foreign learning was curiously limited. The young Chinese intellectual who went abroad to study, or made do with instruction at home (often beginning in a missionary college), concentrated on science, or still more on political economy and political theory. The writings of John Stuart Mill, the exponents of Western democratic ideas, the economists, the scientists were eagerly studied. Very few, by comparison, were interested in European history, poetry or literature. Nor did the great and continuing missionary endeavour bring in many converts to Christianity. Young Chinese attended missionary schools to learn English, the key to further foreign learning. They went abroad to Western universities, but did not read theology. At a time when the thought of the West was at last open to China and in part willingly accepted, the religion of the West, which an earlier generation of Westerners had regarded as the one real contribution that Europe could make, was no more acceptable than it had been to the old conservative scholars. The enthusiastic teachers of Chinese youth, who found them such admirable and intelligent pupils, may have deplored this lapse, but perhaps did not fully understand the reasons behind it.

The Chinese educated class had been converted, suddenly enough, to a realization that European learning was valuable and essential: essential to 'save China'. Not valuable in itself, not necessary for a full and wider understanding of the whole achievement of the human race, but necessary to give back to Chinese the power to compete on equal terms with the West. In a new, more comprehensive way, the urge to acquire Western learning was a form of the older approach, the use of Western learning to preserve Chinese values. It was now understood that mere products of industry without knowledge of the science and technology which lay behind them were useless. It was also seen that the Europeans had more than science and technology: they had political ideas, methods of social control, techniques of government which also contributed mightily to their power. These, too, China must learn, so that China could beat them at their own game.

It is significant that still, half a century later, the Chinese acceptance of Western culture shows these gaps. There are many able scientists in China today; many men have written penetrating works on political science, on economics, some have a great knowledge of European literature. But there are no works produced in China which contribute original research in Western history, there are very few collections of Western art in Chinese museums, and none of any importance. Western works of art are not collected, even by the most wealthy and educated men. There are no journals devoted to European history, archaeology, or art. To most Chinese these branches of Western learning are not of interest. Instinctively it is felt that these things, at least, are better in China. Young modernizers might themselves have little or no appreciation or knowledge of their own art, but they were no more interested in that of Europe than the old scholars. Those aspects of the culture of Europe which had no bearing on China and her prob-

lems, no immediate or ultimate value to the task of re-
building a strong state, had little value for the Chinese
intellectual. It was not, probably, always or often a conscious choice. It was an attitude of mind, shared by a
whole generation and the whole literate class.

This subconscious selection of elements of the Western
culture which were felt to be valuable reflects another
aspect of the adoption of Western civilization by the
Chinese. The conflict between foreign and Chinese values,
the problem of whether to accept and absorb, or to accept
only to make ultimate rejection possible, was not one which
only divided groups or classes: it raged in the minds of
individuals: there are still many indications, even from the
most 'advanced' circles, that the conflict is as yet unre-
solved. Westerners, always conscious of the great cohesive
force of the old Chinese civilization, of its difference from
their own, or any other, used to say that 'China is a sea
which salts all the rivers that flow into it'. A pleasant, cos-
mic image, but one which took no note of what suffering,
mental or physical, the creatures living in this saline water
experienced when subjected to so powerful a flow of fresh
streams.

With a great wrench the young Chinese at the beginning
of this century tore down the old fabric of Chinese institutions. The dynasty was dethroned. Confucius demoted
from his temple; the classical examinations for the civil
service, and with them the whole ancient system of education, were abolished. Democracy, the panacea from the
West, the political system which, so they had been taught,
made the Western nations strong, was now going to save
China. Freed from all the outworn trappings of the Throne,
the Europeans would accept China as an equal, abolish
their Unequal Treaties, renounce their concessions, return
the lost territories. All else would follow. Under democracy
industry would progress, poverty would diminish, military

power would revive. This was the message which hundreds, thousands, of young students had brought back from their studies in Europe and America. They were members of the scholar gentry, the sons and grandsons of the great officials, the natural leaders of the Chinese people. No one seriously questioned their doctrine. Every other had failed. The conservative old scholars could show nothing but decline, weakness, and collapse as the consequence of following their prescriptions.

But then it did not happen. The foreign powers showed little enthusiasm for their new pupil. They preferred the most reactionary military figure they could find, the 'strong man' Yüan Shih-k'ai. He would safeguard their investments. In place of the old, abolished institutions there appeared only yawning gaps, soon filled with very undesirable rubbish. In place of the Emperor there was soon a succession of military adventurers, corrupt and ignorant, very far from adequate Presidents of a Democratic Republic. In place of the old high officials there appeared a swarm of self-seeking careerists, qualified for office only by flagrantly corrupt election or unabashed nepotism. The civil service disintegrated, the military took command, law and order diminished, civil wars between rival commanders swept the country. China's military power, so far from defending the country against its foes, served only to uphold the rule of corruption and to devastate the provinces. This tragic spectacle convinced the foreign observer that the Chinese civilization was at an end, that the long race was run, and since there could be no return to the past, there was equally no future.

One side of the new China was largely ignored by the outside observer, because he was not usually qualified to study it. In the general decay and ruin, education alone prospered. The new universities—the first had been the sole survivor of the abortive reforms of 1898—attracted all the young men who would formerly have studied for the classical examinations of the civil service. They attracted, too, the scholars, the ex-officials; the whole displaced governing class found in the rapidly multiplying new universities a field for their energies, a haven and a career. They were still protected by the aura of reverence which had always surrounded scholarship and learning in China. In the decade following the fall of the dynasty—which happened to coincide with the First World War—the new universities became the one vital, dynamic force in China, cultivating learning old and new, pulsing with new ideas, eagerly debating alternative solutions. Very soon they turned from thought to action: in the years immediately following the First World War the students, particularly those of Peking University, organized political demonstrations which shook the corrupt government of the day and forced it to refrain from some of the more inept and even treasonable activities which its self-seeking members favoured.

This phenomenon was much reprobated by Western observers. They could not understand how students—mere schoolboys even—were permitted to behave like this, meddling with politics, when they should be busy with their studies. How could they know what they were doing, how could they presume to tell their elders they were mistaken? The Chinese had revered age; what had become of the respect for elders? What indeed? But then, who were these elders? They were corrupt adventurers, military despots, ignorant, brutal, and venal. They were not deserving of respect; no one, rich or poor, gave it to them. The students were the sons and descendants of the educated scholar gentry who had ruled China for millennia. They were not themselves responsible for the calamities that had befallen the country in the previous generation, but they were the one class who showed any sign of distress at its

D

present condition, who cared for its future, who were seeking, however clumsily, to find for China a place in the changed world. The Chinese people as a whole did not share the views of foreign observers, but shopkeepers, workmen and, when they were in touch, peasants, came out in support of the students. They, at least, understood.

The impact of the Russian Revolution

It so happened that at this time the ideals of the first generation of advanced reformers were much devalued by events, not only those which were happening in China. The Republic was a failure: democracy a farce. But the Western nations who had seemed so strong and assured had just slaughtered each other on an unprecedented scale, they had overturned many of their own institutions, they had destroyed the unity (fictitious enough, but outwardly presentable) with which they had formerly faced China. From all this had come forth a most significant event, the Russian Revolution.

It is difficult, in the age of the cold war, to recall what impression the Bolsheviks made on the less privileged parts of the world. In China it was immense. Here was seen the most dramatic reversal of fortune. The Russia of the Tsars had been to the Chinese only the most pressing of many enemies, the least subject to any appeal for moderation, the least worthy of emulation, the most reactionary of the European states, which could teach China very little. But as the news, and soon the translated literature, of revolutionary Russia reached China it was suddenly realized that this backward country had jumped right ahead (so it seemed) of the old democratic nations. The new Russia was ready to treat China, and all other weak Asian peoples, as equals: renounce her Unequal Treaties, abolish her concessions, oppose the interventions of other powers, assist China to become once more truly independent and strong. It was true that all this would be better accomplished if the Chinese chose to adopt the Communist programme, which few knew anything about. But the Russians were accommodating; Joffe agreed, and signed his name to a statement, with Sun Yat-sen, acknowledging that 'Communism was not suited to Chinese conditions'. No doubt he added, *sotto voce*, 'not yet'.

At a time when it was not accepted that modern China was making any useful or interesting contribution to learning or thought, those foreigners who were able to read Chinese confined their interest to the records and the literature of the past. They were in any case few: consequently the nature of the movement which now fermented in the universities and overspilled throughout the Chinese educated class passed unnoticed. It was not known that hardly a novel or a piece of literature, essay or political tract was published that was not inspired with Left opinions, if not yet specifically Communist (for Marxism was hardly known except in outline) yet shot through with the assumptions of the Left, critical and hostile to the capitalist world, contemptuous of the democratic system which the former generation had so ardently admired. The groundwork for Communism was already well prepared before ever there was a Communist Party in China, but when it was formed, it rapidly spread its message among the educated.

Chinese Communism

The Chinese Communist Party was formed with some eight members in 1921. By 1924 it was already treating with Dr Sun Yat-sen's Nationalist Party on nearly equal terms; two years later it was spearheading the Northern Expedition to oust the militarist régimes and dominating the new revolutionary government in Hankow. Yet it was also a very 'infantile' party, held in leading-strings by Russian advisers, led by young, inexperienced returned students. Many years of adversity and changing fortunes lay before it; for a long time it only appealed to a minority and the mass of the educated class were willing to follow Nationalist leadership in their search for the programme and party which would restore China. It was only the mistakes and the failings of that leadership which slowly turned its following away. The essential character of this long internal struggle, fought not only in the field but also in the minds of men, was the question of which method could best achieve the end which both sides sought to reach, the restoration of China. It is really open to doubt whether many on either side were more wedded to the means than the end, whether they valued doctrine and principle above power, whether they cared more for form than for content.

For the Chinese had not forgotten the teaching of so many centuries, which had always stressed the importance of behaviour and minimized the value of theory. The Mandate of Heaven, that right to rule which the old Chinese recognized as conferring legitimacy on a government, was based on the simple proposition that if one contestant proved stronger than the other, the Mandate had passed to the victor. The Chinese are a very practical people. The ends which they were seeking to attain were reached within a few years of the final triumph of the Communist Party; therefore that party had acquired the 'Mandate', the rights of the successful.

It has often been pointed out that Communism should not appeal to the Chinese people: they are individualistic, they are natural traders, money-makers, land hungry, and capitalist in their instincts. They put the family before the state; they did not co-operate closely with men of another kin; in short they were well suited to a system of free enterprise, the freer the better. It is also true that these characteristics are mostly condemned and repressed by the system now prevailing in China. Individualism is a sin, very much reprobated and constantly denounced; which does indeed go far to proving that it is in fact very prevalent. The economy as now organized leaves very little room for private business, trade, money-making, or financial operations. Land has been collectivized, and private ownership of agricultural land (as opposed to house property on a limited scale) no longer exists. Legislation and social pressures have reduced the old extended families to the point where they are no longer real social units: the modern Chinese family is the biological family of parents and children. The Chinese have been led and guided into systems of co-operation with each other which are not only not family or kin groups, but take great care to avoid any identification with kin or even regional affiliations.

These are major changes; however much the strength of the state has been restored, the economy rehabilitated, the national morale lifted, it is still clear that the Chinese Communist Party has not merely 'restored the rule of the T'ang'—revived the Chinese Empire in new guise: it has also reshaped it on very different lines. How far this new system is really so much opposed to abiding Chinese traditions, and not merely to habits formed in the recent period of decline and confusion, can be disputed, but it is becoming more and more clear that the internal transformation of society, however thorough, has much less significance for the relationship between China and the rest of the world than was at first expected. The Chinese Communists themselves have finally buried the notion, cherished by their opponents, that the People's Republic and the Communist Party were nothing but the agents of Russia, subjecting China to the dictates of Moscow. The alternative possibility, that the Chinese still retain their former view of the world and their place in it, can be supported by positive evidence and deserves examination.

Doctrinal claims

In the first years of their rule the Chinese Communist Party seemed to go out of their way to substantiate the charges of their enemies. They openly proclaimed that in international affairs they leaned to one side, the side of Russia. They praised the achievements of the U.S.S.R., declared that Russia was the only valid model on which the Chinese state could be rebuilt, and acknowledged Russia as the leader of the 'socialist camp', the prime exemplar and guide on the road to Communism. But at that time China was very weak, believing herself to be directly menaced by American hostility and with no other friend to whom she could turn. It was not long before the tone of Chinese pronouncements began to change. As far back as 1949 Liu Shao-ch'i, in a speech to the W.F.T.U. Conference in Peking, claimed that their revolution was the model for the underdeveloped, or 'semi-colonial' countries. Mao Tse-tung had added to the 'treasury of Marxist-Leninist thought', a claim never made by any other Communist leader, and barely admitted, if at all, by the Russian leadership.[1]

The implications of such a claim were deep. If China had provided the model on which future revolutions among the peoples of Asia (and perhaps later of Africa) should be based, this was also a claim that China should lead and guide these revolutions towards their goal: the claim that Mao had added new truths to Marxism, meaning the experience and practice of the Chinese revolution, was also

[1] Speech of Lu Ting-yi, member of the Central Committee of the CCP, 25 June 1951.

a claim that China could provide that interpretation of the orthodox doctrines of Communism most applicable in her region. These arguments amounted to a restatement in modern terms of two of the fundamental postulates of the old Chinese view of the world: that China was the centre of civilization, the model which less advanced states and peoples should copy if they were to be accepted within the pale, and that the ruler of China was the expounder of orthodox doctrine; that, after all and always, Chinese interpretations were the right ones; truth and right thinking must come from China and conform with Chinese teaching.

In the days of weakness and decline the Chinese had for a time almost doubted this: the 'Young China' generation of the first decade of the twentieth century had turned away from what seemed a worn-out tradition and had wholeheartedly sought in the West a doctrine which would suit the changed modern world, and once more restore China to her rightful place. Now they had found it: Marxism might be of foreign origin, but Mao Tse-tung was most certainly a pure Chinese, had never even studied abroad, knew no foreign language. His thought was Chinese, and when applied to Marxism that teaching was thereby incorporated in the new Chinese tradition. This was not altogether an easy proposition; it could not be, and was not at first made too explicit. China was growing stronger, but was still dependent on her Russian ally. But as the years passed and the reorganization of China, the rise of her new industries, the growth of her military power became more and more assured, the new interpretation became clearer and was expressed more freely. In 1956 the engineering projects and constructions which covered the face of China were still openly and officially credited to the plans and work of the 'Soviet comrades'. But already it was also said that 'China did not have to copy Soviet methods in all matters, for Chinese conditions were different'. It was also being said that 'China can learn from Soviet mistakes'. Two years later, in 1958, it was being said, and of the same projects and constructions, that 'although the original plans were drawn up by the Soviet comrades, engineer Wu, or Professor Chang, improved upon them, and it was these improved plans which we have carried out'.

Chinese isolation

In that same year the Communes were established and announced as a short cut to Communism, claimed as an advance which no other Socialist country had yet attempted. It is well known that this claim was derided by the Russians: the subsequent partial failure of the Commune experiment and retreat from the more lofty aims which it had been hoped they would reach, seemed to confirm the correctness of the Russian judgement. It is also clear that it was at least in large part this difference of view over the Communes, and the subsequent withdrawal of much Soviet technical aid, which initiated the growing divergence of policy between China and Russia, which in later years broke out into open recrimination. The withdrawal of many Soviet advisers and technicians was, in reality, already beginning in 1958, before the Commune experiment had really got under way. They were being replaced by East Germans, and little attempt was then made to conceal the fact that this change was due to the humbler position which such East Germans had to occupy. Coming from a country which was barely independent, powerless, and subservient, the East Germans did what they were told and did it well. They did not argue with the Chinese, they did not, could not, use the influence of their home government to press their views. They made excellent servants.

It was also in the year 1958 that China made her most

serious and sustained effort to recover the Offshore Islands still under Nationalist control. American arms were freely supplied to the Nationalist defenders, including guided missiles from aircraft (sidewinders) which proved deadly to the Chinese Communist aircraft. Russia did not supply China with similar devices, and, it is now known, positively refused to give China anything more than verbal support in this crisis. China was forced to desist and the struggle for the islands dwindled to desultory shelling and then died away. The one, true ally had not proved willing to take any risks: Mr Khrushchev visited the United States and conferred, amicably enough, with President Eisenhower at Camp David.

The impression which this expedition made upon China can be compared with the effect which would be produced in America if Mr Macmillan, in the present year, were to pay a friendly visit to Fidel Castro. It was inexplicable in terms of good faith and true friendship; it was very near to treason; it was folly and weakness. America was, and is, to China enemy number one. America has refused to recognize Peking, has supported and allied herself with Chiang K'ai-shek (in Chinese eyes a dissident rebel), blocks China's claim to her seat at the United Nations, continues, no matter which party controls the administration, to take a hostile stance, to exclude China as much as possible, to impose a trade embargo, travel bans, and all other hostile actions short of war. If alliance with Russia means that Russia is free to confer with the enemy, to refuse support to China when it is Chinese interests which are in question, but to further her own when opportunity offers, even at China's expense, then the Chinese may well ask, what is the value of an alliance?

The Chinese have never had much experience of alliances. Living in their own world, in which they were long supreme, their relations with such other organized states as from time to time existed in their vicinity were either hostile, or those of suzerain to tributary. Large powers such as the Tatar Liao in North China in the Sung period, or their Mongol successors, were enemies. Small powers, such as Korea or Annam, were tributaries. Japan was claimed to be in this class, and later, when the claim could not be substantiated, became an enemy. There was never an ally of equal standing. In the nineteenth century, when China was reluctantly forced into a new world of powers and sovereign states too distant to be treated as tributaries, too strong to be ignored, her policy was to 'play off one barbarian against another', to strive by working on the jealousies and greed of the Western powers to set them against each other, to get one to frustrate the schemes of a rival. Up to a point this policy gave results. France, Germany, and Russia were used to oust Japan from south Manchuria where she had won spoils by defeating China in the war of 1895. But a large part of the recovered territory, and far-reaching concessions, had to be paid as the price to the Russians themselves. France also got her compensation in the south. It was the policy of the bankrupt, borrowing from one source to fend off the too pressing claims of another creditor, only ultimately involving further loss and deeper debt.

During all this period the Chinese Court never concluded an alliance with any other power. It may be that had they tried, they would not have found it so very easy to find a friend. But they did not try; they never envisaged foreign policy in terms of alliances, of balance of power. The old, rooted outlook, that China was the supreme central empire needing no friend, having no neighbour worthy to be an ally, an equal, held fast. Japan could win an alliance with Britain which greatly helped her rise: but Japan, in Chinese eyes, was an inferior state. Her success in war and her growth in industry could not alter this established fact. Japanese culture owed much to borrowing from China, many centuries earlier, in the T'ang period. Therefore Japan had been a country irradiated by Chinese civilization. She could not be a model, or an equal, any more than the moon can be the equal of the sun.

When the Republic was established the Chinese of the revolutionary party certainly expected to gain the goodwill of the democratic states, and especially of the United States, but they did not try to confirm this by seeking an alliance with any power. The United States would not at that time enter into alliances with foreign states; Britain was in Chinese eyes, even though democratic, the foremost of the imperialist powers in the East. France was little better. The Chinese, during the First World War, had much sympathy for Germany, mainly because she was at war with Britain and France, the old assailants of China. Under very strong pressure from the Allied Powers, the weak Chinese government was finally forced to break off relations with Germany and become their 'ally'. This was seen in China as a piece of bullying, from which they derived no profit, and were, at Versailles, even cheated out of their own territory of Tsingtao, the ex-German concessionary port, which was awarded to Japan. Such were the fruits of this unwelcome 'alliance' of the First World War.

This first experience of being an ally did not therefore predispose the Chinese to take a new view of foreign relations. When they had been strong they had needed no ally, when they were weak, allies had proved to be false friends. It is, of course, only too clear that the warlord-ridden feeble government of China in the period of the First World War was not a useful ally to the belligerent powers; all they wanted was to lay hands on the German shipping harbouring in Chinese ports. Later they found Chinese labour useful on the Western Front. An unexpected by-product of the employment of such labour was that several young students went as interpreters with the labourers, and some of these stayed in France to study, where they learned about Communism. One of them was Chou En-lai.

When the Nationalist Party gained control of most of China, after 1927, there was for the first time since the death of Yüan Shih-k'ai a government which could be seriously regarded as the government of all China. The foreign powers had been unwilling to deal with Dr Sun Yat-sen's régime when it only held Canton. By 1927 some of the foreign powers at least were beginning to be alarmed at the ambitions of Japan, and all the Western powers felt deep suspicion of Soviet Russia. The Russians had backed the Chinese revolutionary movement in 1926 when it had swept the warlords out of power, but after the split between Nationalists and Communists in the following year, the new Nationalist régime in Nanking was bitterly anti-Communist. This, however, did not make it turn to the foreign powers to seek an alliance.

The foreign policy of the Nanking government was to seek to abolish the Unequal Treaties, and its internal policy was a sustained but fruitless effort to quell the Communist uprising. The Russians no longer had any Unequal Treaty with China, but as the sponsors of the Communist Party they were anathema to the Nanking government, which therefore sought no pact with them. The Western democracies were the beneficiaries of the Unequal Treaties, and as such, engaged in a diplomatic defensive to withstand Chinese pressure for the abolition of these treaties. No alliance was sought from them. Japan was, ever more clearly, the dangerous enemy of China, against whom, by all the rules of foreign policy, China should have looked for a strong ally. But China relied on the League of Nations: America was isolationist and made no foreign alliances, the European powers, afraid of Japan, and pre-occupied by the reviving German danger, wanted no involvements in the Far East. China faced Japan without a friend.

As a result, when Japan moved to the attack, China got only words from the West, and resolutions condemning aggression (well watered down) from the League of Nations. Appeasement of Japan, although not known by that unpopular term, continued to be the policy of the Western powers after the war with Germany had broken out. The United States, still neutral, followed the same path. China got little help in her lonely struggle: the Burma road, her one safe supply line, was temporarily closed for three months. When the Japanese, still unappeased, struck at Pearl Harbour and simultaneously invaded Malaya and the Netherlands East Indies, China suddenly, overnight, acquired powerful allies, but not by any will of their own. For three years this did China no good. The allies were defeated, driven from the Philippines, Malaya, the East Indies, and Burma.

Ultimately the allies won the war, Japan surrendered, and withdrew from China. By that time China was already about to be engulfed in the final civil war between the Communists and Nationalists. The consequence of the victory of the Communists was that the United States, the only Western power which still counted in the Far East, ceased to be an ally of the new régime and became its declared enemy; soon the supporter of the fallen Chiang K'ai-shek, who established himself in Formosa, sheltered under American protection. No lasting or valuable alliance had come from the fortuitous partnerships into which Japanese aggressions had forced China and the West. These were the only alliances that the Chinese state had ever entertained. They did not represent a line of foreign policy, but ran counter to the policy which had been pursued in peacetime: they were accidental, and proved ephemeral.

The alliance with Soviet Russia into which the new Communist government formally entered soon after it was established in 1949 was thus the first deliberately chosen alliance in Chinese history. It was soon to be tested in the Korean War. It is usually now accepted that China was not a party to the outbreak of that war, which there is some evidence to show caught the Peking government by surprise. But the area of operations was one of vital interest to China, bordering upon Manchuria, the one (although partly dismantled) industrial region in China which had been extensively developed. When the advance of General MacArthur's forces brought them close to the Yalu river, the frontier, China intervened, describing her forces as 'volunteers', and drove the United Nations' forces back beyond Seoul. Russia made no move. Although China now had an ally, when it came to what the Chinese saw as a threat to their national interests, the approach of a hostile army to their frontier, and the prospect of a hostile occupation of an area which dominated their essential industrial region, they were left to defend it with their own forces alone, although these 'volunteers' received Soviet arms and equipment. To everyone's surprise they did so very effectively. Yet to many Chinese this experience must have called in question the real value of the new alliance just as much as previous history had cast doubt on the quality of earlier allies.

For several years if such doubts were felt among the leadership, they were never allowed to appear in print. Officially China and Russia remained firm friends, but it was more than once suggested by Western observers that in some matters concerning this friendship Russia did 'protest too much'. Whenever the question of China's seat at the United Nations came up, Russia vigorously took the part of Peking, made loud discourteous protests, levelled accusations right and left, and in other ways seemed intent on creating the maximum amount of opposition to this proposal. As the acceptance of Peking was made to appear possible only by conceding an outright diplomatic victory to the Soviet Union, American opposition to any such plan hardened, and pressure was put upon all states seeking American goodwill to keep in line with the United States. The various proposals were, year after year, invariably and easily defeated. Alone among the Western powers Britain recognized the Peking government and continued to maintain diplomatic relations with it, albeit at Chinese insistence only on the level of chargé d'affaires. With this solitary exception China has no relations with any major power other than the U.S.S.R. The foreign relations of the People's Republic are thus almost as limited as those of the Manchu Empire: aloof, formal relations with powers which are not very friendly, a closer tie with a number of weak or distant states of similar outlook (Communist countries of Eastern Europe), and, the one exception, an overt alliance with the Soviet Union. To these must be added relations with the newly independent states of Asia, and later some in Africa.

The dispute with Russia

This pattern gives the Chinese government very little scope in foreign relations and tends to emphasize the sense of isolation. It also reinforces the traditional Chinese view of the world, which sees China as the centre, the sole upholder of true civilization, the lawgiver to the barbarians. There can be now no doubt that this view, in a modern form, is prevalent in China and is positively stated in the many polemical articles which have appeared since the dispute with the Soviet Union has come into the open.

The Chinese now claim to be the upholders of pure Marx-ism, and denounce Russia as faint-hearted, 'revisionist', and too ready, for fear of nuclear war, to betray world revolution in favour of a form of coexistence which would in reality lead to the perpetuation of the capitalist society. China, on the contrary, is not afraid of the 'paper tigers' of imperialism, is ready to step in and support revolutionary wars, and while not seeking to provoke a wider, nuclear, conflict, maintains that the risk must be run if the world revolution is to go forward. Wars are won by men, not weapons alone.[1] China has the men; she also has the courage, the true doctrine, and will therefore get the sup-port of the working class of the whole world, and thus is best fitted for the leadership of the future world Com-munist society.

Stated thus it can be clearly seen that this claim is very close to the old Chinese outlook, with some changes which history may well come to see as superficial. Marx has re-placed Confucius, but it is Mao Tse-tung who interprets the teachings of the Master. The new emphasis is more on power, material strength, than the old stress on moral excellence. The Chinese do not now say, as the old Con-fucians did, that the true ruler needs no armies, for the barbarians and foreigners will be attracted to him by the very virtue of his government. The modern claim still, indeed, implies that the purity of Chinese Marxism will attract and convince the working class of the world, but part of the criticism of Russia is directed against the view that the 'inevitable' success of the Communist system will in itself convert the world, and that great revolutionary wars are no longer necessary. It may be that the modern Chinese, taking note of the very real limitations in the

[1] Among numerous recent statements of this view see in particular *Hongqi* (Red Flag), Editorial Dept., *More on the Differences between Comrade Togliatti and Us* (Peking, Foreign Language Press, 4 March 1963).

application of the old Confucian theory, have decided
that purity of doctrine is not enough: armed force may
often be needed to establish the rule of true doctrine. It
must be added that many a Confucian Emperor was of
this opinion too, and acted on it.

If this wordy debate were confined to scholiasts of Marxism, and had no immediate bearing on the conduct of
policy, it would be of interest to the historian of ideas, but
only of marginal importance to the statesman. It therefore
becomes important to determine whether the dispute is
academic or real; and if real, what are the true problems
underlying it. Leaving aside the relative purity or con-
tamination of the Marxism practised in Peking and in
Moscow, it is clear that there is a very real question at
issue. Should the fear of nuclear catastrophe cause the
Communist world to change its goals, as well as its methods:
or is this fear exaggerated, ultimately unreal, and therefore not to be allowed overriding weight in determining
the course of policy? There is also the corollary, that if it
is true that revolution is the only road by which Communism can come to power, then revolutionary wars should be
supported by devoted Communists, even at great risk.

Khrushchev has pointed out that the imperialist paper
tigers still have nuclear claws. The Chinese argue that
they will never dare to use them. The Russians, as Cuba
has shown, are acutely aware that the support of revolutionary wars can lead to a confrontation of the major
antagonists, and that this is too high a price to pay. The
Chinese deny this, but are not themselves really willing to
practise what they preach. In southern Vietnam there is
now what must by any definition agree with the description 'revolutionary war'. A large Communist insurrection
is waging guerrilla war, with much success, against a rather
reactionary government which is sustained by American
support stopping only just short of military intervention.

E

The Chinese, according to their own doctrine, ought then to be themselves openly engaged in this conflict. It greatly resembles the struggle of fifteen years ago in China itself. It is, of course, true that then Russia, the Communist neighbour, did not openly support the Chinese Communists, nor did she give them clandestine assistance, any more than China is now giving such assistance to the Viet Cong.

Russian failure to support the Chinese communists could be cited by the Chinese as early evidence of Russian timidity in the great cause, but they have not yet done so. While praising the heroic struggles of the people of Vietnam, the Chinese government has made no open move on their behalf. This would seem to be wisdom, for such a move would bring China so close to conflict with American forces that a wider war might not be averted. Yet this consideration, in the case of Cuba, is just what the Chinese regard as faintheartedness on the part of the Russians. In Laos the Chinese were also prepared to negotiate with the arch-enemy to establish, not the triumph of the Communist-led Pathet Lao, but the neutralization of the whole state, and its removal, if possible, from the arena of cold war. This was an exercise in the practice of coexistence; some might say it was also an abandonment of a revolutionary cause, but it may well be regarded as only a temporary expedient.

Vietnam and Laos are near to China, Cuba is far away. The argument that circumstances alter cases, that theory is one thing, but practice must often be another, is the Russian, not the Chinese, argument in this dispute; but it is seemingly the view taken in Peking when it comes to acts rather than words, Here there appears a characteristic familiar from the history of Imperial China. The Emperor never failed to proclaim his adherence to the letter of Confucian orthodoxy: his acts of state were supposed, and declared, to be wholly consonant with true doctrine. But Chinese historians, and, one must suppose contemporaries also, were perfectly well aware that this was often a polite fiction. The prevalence of such fictions was one of the aspects of Chinese life and thought which Western observers found least attractive. The attitude of mind which lay behind the practice was not familiar to the West, and was misunderstood.

The Christian from the West is prepared to denounce himself as a 'miserable sinner'. A Chinese considered that he, and all men, should have 'a sense of shame'. But there is a wide and deep difference between sin and shame. The Chinese did not have the sense of sin, and in their view the European seemed often to lack the sense of shame. To confess to wicked and evil actions, thoughts, or intentions is a sign of Christian humility and repentance. To the Chinese an admission that evil had been ever preferred to virtue, that even if weak and incapable, man had not always striven for the best, would be indeed shameless. It would imply that there was in human nature some inherent defect, when in the Chinese understanding, man was born good and blameless and if he did not remain so, it was from neglect, from a failure to cultivate his natural virtue, not from the growth of his natural vice. The nature of man, said one of the great Sung philosophers, is like a mirror covered with dust: wipe away the dust of neglect and the true surface of the mirror appears as bright as ever.

This being the fundamental postulate it follows that the path of virtue must always be followed, and if in fact lost, it must at least be never admitted that such a thing could happen. That would be to lack a sense of shame. Shame is the goad which keeps men on the right track, and at the very least impels them to proclaim their devotion to virtue. To do otherwise would be the true 'loss of face', undignified, derogating from the status of a human being. The difference in standpoint is basic, and explains many aspects of the Chinese character.

What must be said, and what can be done, need not therefore agree. The true doctrine must always be proclaimed; to admit openly that in some circumstances it cannot be applied is not only humiliating—shameful—but utterly wrong, for it sets a bad example, allowing the ignorant to suspect that virtue will not always triumph, suggesting that there are in fact alternative doctrines valid in some cases, and thus impugning the perfection of true orthodoxy. For the Russians to admit the power of the 'imperialists', to suggest that it is so great as to deter Communists from doing what they ought to do, is a terrible heresy. It implies that Communism (true doctrine) is not always certain of victory. But if that were so, in the Chinese view, then Communism could not be true doctrine, for by definition the nature of the universe is good, and the triumph of truth and virtue a law of that universe.

The Chinese may not be able to practise the full rigours of the true doctrine when it has to be applied to situations such as South Vietnam, but they would think it monstrous to say so. Such a confession would discourage revolutionaries everywhere, would imply a failure of morale, a conscious, and therefore at bottom, a willing acceptance of the wrong doctrine. The Chinese anger at the public criticism of 'fraternal parties'—the Albanians and themselves—stems from the same outlook. It is outrageous to state in public that anyone else is a rank offender. It inflicts loss of face, and in old China such conduct would lead to a deadly and undying feud. The Chinese Communists may denounce 'face' as a 'feudal' convention, just as the Russian Communists may repudiate the Christian idea of sin, but both communities are still built upon the old cultural traditions of the past and cannot rid themselves of their inherited national viewpoints.

If the Chinese claims are examined in the light of this
traditional approach, they may appear less menacing.
'Pure Marxism' must of course be adhered to, announced,
and published to the world. Contrasts between what is said
and what is done should be concealed. Any other course
can only weaken the Communist movement, encourage
its foes, and divide the faithful. Moreover the time for compromise, if it ever should be necessary, is not now, and
compromise should at best be a temporary expedient; it
must indeed be such, for in the end Communism (Virtue)
must prevail. This does not mean that reckless adventures
are to be encouraged, but only that heroic actions should
be held up as an example, not called 'adventurism'.

If the Chinese Communist Party is thus making a claim
to be better Marxists than the Russians, more fitted to lead
the Communist world, and ultimately to lead it to total
victory, this programme is clearly a long way from being
realized, is indeed theoretical rather than a blueprint for
a policy which can be carried out. Russia does not concede
this primacy: it is Russia which has the nuclear weapons;
China has not yet won the support of most of the Communist Parties of the Western world. She has the Korean,
Indonesian, and Burmese parties lined up on her side.
Other Asian parties such as the Malayan and Vietnamese
are still displaying indecision. In other words, the ideological alignment of Communist parties represents very
clearly the outline of the military power and political influence of the Russian and the Chinese states. In Korea,
where Chinese arms were deployed to save the North
Korean régime, her leadership is accepted, as it had better
be. North Vietnam may feel more secure, but its hopes of
bringing the southern Vietnamese revolution to victory
largely depend on Chinese support. So North Vietnam
tries to sit on the fence and make peace between her
quarrelling friends. Eastern and Western Europe, with

dissident Albania as the exception, follow the Russian lead. It is the most 'Western' parties, the French and Italian, who have criticized the Chinese most sharply. The outlook of Communist parties seems often to be motivated by racial backgrounds, just as much as are the views of conservative parties.

Motives for the dispute

Since the Chinese cannot at present convince their supposed friends, and make no progress in winning new ones, the reasons for raising so great a dispute seem inadequate. It could be supposed that China, isolated by the continuing hostility of America, repelled by her Communist colleagues, and now at odds with the leading non-aligned power, India, has fallen back into a new version of the old unreal view of the world, such as prevailed in the first half of the nineteenth century. But there is another possible explanation. Behind the theoretical dispute about Marxist purity and revolutionary wars lies the concrete fact that Russia and China in the view of the Western powers are not in the same situation. Russia may be the feared opponent of the West, but she is a recognized power; no settlement of the great disputes existing in different parts of the world can be made without Russian participation. In recent years Russia has seemed more willing to negotiate, perhaps to compromise. It is natural that the Chinese should fear that any such compromise may be made at their expense.

China stands almost alone. She is excluded from the United Nations, only a minority of the major powers recognize her government, whole continents, such as South America, take the opposite line. Except for the conferences dealing with Korea, Laos, and North Vietnam China has been called to no meeting of the world powers and is indeed systematically excluded from them. The evidence has been so far that Russia will always make an escape for herself and leave China to face the consequences. It was so in Korea: when the Korean War (which Russia, not China, started) went badly for her North Korean protégés, it was China, now herself menaced (or sincerely believing that she was) who had to intervene. It was only when Stalin was dead that the war could be brought to an end, and there is some reason to think that he had deliberately involved Mao Tse-tung in the Korean War in the hope of ridding himself of a too independent competitor. The Chinese did not get the arms they needed from Russia in the Offshore Islands crisis of 1958. After the Communes had been established Russia began to withdraw her technical assistance, and in the depths of the bad years 1959–61 ceased her economic assistance also. This is not a record which can make the Chinese confident of the value of the Russian alliance.

There is, therefore, good reason for the Chinese to fear that the Russians might make a deal with the West behind their backs, and that part of the terms of such a deal would be a betrayal of Chinese interests. These interests are clearly not going to be defended by her avowed opponent, America, or safeguarded by the intervention of other non-Communist powers. The purpose of China's high claims at this time may therefore be to assume, in the face of Russian tendencies to accommodation, an unyielding attitude which will make it difficult for such a deal to be carried out without dividing the Communist world and thus gravely weakening Russia herself. The immense interest which China's statement of her case in her leading journals has evoked in the country itself, the evident deep response which the Chinese people feel for this new assertion of an ancient pride, show that there are other calculations at work. After the lean years of the Commune experiment and the failure of the Great Leap Forward, the régime needed a policy which was truly popular; denouncing the foreigner has always been a sure means of arousing popular enthusiasm, and when this is coupled with a restatement of China's traditional standpoint, it is all the more certain to be greeted with wholehearted approval.

The Chinese people have some cause to think that their rulers are in the right. For all but the oldest generation their memories are of the chaos and misery of the warlord period, the corruption and weakness of the Nationalist régime, followed by the Japanese invasion. Then came the Communists, and since then China has been restored to ordered government, an advancing economy, national power and prestige. To a large generation of the young this last phase is their real experience, and it has been an intensely stimulating one. They see the outside world as either openly hostile, covertly opposed, or jealous of China's rise. This causes no surprise, for the Chinese had little reason to think that they had friends abroad before, and had never expected to find any. They remain convinced that their new way is as superior to all competing ways as they were formerly convinced that the Confucian Empire was superior to the barbarians.

This is not an attitude of mind which makes the working of an alliance smooth. In the habits and practices of dealing with equals China has had very little experience, but it would probably be a mistake to conclude that the sharpness of the present dispute with Russia is the prelude to a rupture of their formal alliance and a complete break. It may be convenient, at home, to take once more the high tone of the imperial decrees, proclaiming virtue and China's faithful support of the true doctrine: but the more practical aim of keeping Russia from engaging in manoeuvres detrimental to China suggests that the Chinese leadership are well aware that real isolation would be dangerous, however psychologically satisfying to Chinese pride. Moreover, if China is to win an equal, let alone the foremost place in the Communist world, she must remain a member of it. The risks have been calculated, and it is improbable that the risk of a total rupture with Russia was rated high.

For in one respect the Chinese estimation of the Western 'imperialists' as 'paper tigers' may not be so far astray. Although China and Russia have been openly in dispute for three years, no Western initiative to profit by this development has yet appeared. The American stand against China remains as rigid as it did in the days of Mr Dulles, if less luridly announced. Although the thesis supported by the former Secretary for State, that China was but the 'instrument of international Communism', the tool of Russia, is manifestly disproved, no new policy has been adopted. It would seem that, as far as the West is concerned, China and Russia may quarrel to their hearts content, without provoking any move from the West. Nor does it seem likely that this inertia proceeds from subtle calculation that, given time, the Russo-Chinese dispute will disrupt the Communist world. It derives, all too clearly, from the rigid bonds of commitments made to Chiang K'ai-shek in the days when it was held as an article of faith that the Communist régime in China would soon be overthrown and the Nationalists restored. The Chinese know well that they will not be wooed by America, and there is nothing to be obtained from taking a conciliatory attitude towards the West. They have reason to believe that force and power will be respected but weakness will be exploited and ignored. There is clear evidence that only the possession of nuclear weapons on a sufficient scale to act as a real deterrent can win for any nation in the contemporary world a place among the final arbiters of war and peace, the real standing of a Great Power.

China can, by the size of her population and her potential resources, in time win such a place, and it is likely that her policy is directed to this end as the immediate objective. Once admitted to be a dangerous nuclear power she could deal with Russia on a basis of equality, could wring from the reluctant West acceptance of her status, and could then, but not till then, consider the advantages of a more co-operative attitude to her Communist allies and a more moderate tone to her capitalist opponents. What her policy must seek to avoid is the kind of settlement which would leave her permanently in the second rank, for their experience in recent years and long history alike have conditioned the Chinese to believe that supreme power is their heritage and that any inferior status is but the prelude to further decline.

The aims of foreign policy

There are in the present Chinese foreign policy, and behind that in the outlook of the Chinese Communist Party, two unreconciled and divergent aims. The first, to regain the full territory and standing of the Chinese Empire at its peak, is the continuation of the movement to 'revive China' which actuated the early revolutionaries and reformers. It makes equal appeal to all Chinese, of the party, against the party, or without party. It is therefore a force for national unification, and one which tends to draw the sting of opposition criticism. It is the drive behind such demonstrations as the Sino-Indian border dispute, seen by Chinese (everywhere) as a just claim to lost lands. But policies designed to implement this aim conflict with those which seek to assert Chinese moral and material leadership in the Communist movement and beyond it. The quarrel with India, whether partly justified or not, may have alienated some of China's Asian neighbours.

The continuing hostility to America, and still more the
violence of the language used in expressing it, are not
calculated to further Chinese policy, even if this policy is
ideologically 'correct'. The quarrel with the United States
is essentially ideological: neither power seeks to obtain, or
retain, part of the other's territory. It is true that the
Chinese see American support of Chiang as an intrusion
into China's internal affairs, a deliberate attempt to keep
China divided, and to retain Taiwan under a régime
dependent on American power. But this situation springs
from American opposition to Communism, not to a belief
that Taiwan is not rightfully Chinese territory. In spite of
the fact that the island is still, in international law, neither
Chinese nor Japanese, the American government recog-
nizes the government on it as the government of the Republic of China.

A less rigid attitude on this question by the Chinese
Communists would bring out the inconsistency of the
present American policy. If the real reason for supporting
Chiang was to oppose any extension of 'international
Communism', by which was meant the power and influence of the Soviet Union, then, now that it is evident
that Communism is ceasing to be so 'international', it
might be thought that there would be room for some form
of accommodation or settlement, or at least for some effort
to explore the possibility of settlement. Neither side makes
any such approach. If the West has done nothing to ex-
ploit the differences between China and Russia, the Chinese
have been equally unwilling—or unable—to use this situation to further their own policies. Chinese local aims, the
restoration of the old empire's full power and status in the
Far East, cannot be achieved in the face of American
opposition in Taiwan, South Vietnam, or South Korea.
China's wider purpose of winning the leadership of the
Communist world and the support of the revolutionary

movements in the undeveloped countries cannot be attained if her dispute with Russia is conducted in such a way as to disrupt the unity of the Communist movement and isolate herself.

The two conflicting urges are, in their present form, the later expressions of the old problem which confronted the Chinese when in the nineteenth century they were forced to recognize that the Confucian Empire as then organized was no longer an adequate response to the changed world situation. 'Chinese learning as the basic structure, Western learning for use', advised the great viceroy and scholar Chang Chih-tung. The other moderate reformers took this saying as their guide. But the revolutionaries decided that it was inadequate. It was necessary to absorb the Western learning, not merely for use but as the real foundation on which China could be restored. The dispute has never really ended. To some the Communist system is, clearly, 'Western learning for use'. It is a system which can restore the strength of China, but for Chinese ends, not for the benefit of the 'working class of the world' or anyone else. It has made China strong, enabled her to recover much lost ground, may enable her to establish a new, far wider Chinese domination and leadership, built upon the other side of the proposition, the fundamental superiority of the Chinese way of thought and tradition—'Chinese learning' as now understood.

To the heirs of the revolutionary movement this is heresy: they would still believe that China must and can absorb the Western teaching, the one that has proved most adequate to her needs, which in their view is Communism. On this new basis China can be revived and restored, but this restoration should only be a part of a great world movement to establish the Communist system in every country. They would agree with others in foreseeing for China a major role in this process, and a high place among the peoples that will control it. The evidence of the continuing dispute with Russia, the means taken to deal with the Indian frontier question, suggest that it is the tendency to see the problem as 'Chinese learning as the base, Western learning for use' which is gradually gaining strength. Isolation and outside hostility reinforce the trend towards nationalist feeling; the meagre results of pursuing a policy of close alliance with the Soviet Union, the manifest unwillingness of Russia to hazard her own interests on China's behalf, all strengthen the pull of the old tradition. That tradition did not rely upon or expect assistance from foreign powers, but saw all 'Western learning' as a repository of skills and techniques from which China could select and adapt those most useful to her, while ignoring the rest and basing her outlook upon the trusted and ancient concepts of Chinese learning.

This need not and will not mean a return to Confucian thought: the modern sees that that philosophy and the society it sustained were inadequate, not in fact truly 'Chinese' since it applied only to a part of the Chinese people, the rich and educated. The great emphasis put today on popular traditions, arts, and customs stems from the belief that these enshrine the true, universal culture of the Chinese race, the real base of 'Chinese learning' on which the sound society can be constructed. The fact that this also agrees with the doctrines of Communism confirms the view that Communism is the Western teaching most suited for China: but the outlook is centred on the needs and desires of China and the Chinese people, not on the more hypothetical requirements of the working classes of the world.

The Chinese view of the world has not fundamentally changed: it has been adjusted to take account of the modern world, but only so far as to permit China to occupy, still, the central place in the picture. To do this it was necessary to accept from the West a new doctrine to replace the inadequate Confucian teaching, which was too limited. After a long struggle China found that the doctrine which suited her was the one which the West had repudiated: and it may well be that this in itself was a reason for making Communism, the outcast of Western origin, welcome in China. It was more easily digestible, could be assimilated to Chinese ways without bringing with it the full force of the Western influences. What was not possible was for China to continue for long to acknowledge the debt, and accept the position of pupil. Mao Tsetung had to 'enrich the treasury of Marxist-Leninist thought', so that the contents of that treasury could become current coin in China; it was inevitable that Chinese Marxism should be found to be purer than that of Russia, that Mao should be hailed as the greater prophet, and that 'some people' should be shown to be in error. There cannot be two suns in one sky.